Goliath Bird-Eating Tarantula

The World's Biggest Spider

by Meish Goldish

Consultant: Meredith Whitney
Herpetology and Conservation Manager
The Maryland Zoo in Baltimore
Baltimore, MD

BEARPORT
PUBLISHING

New York, New York

Credits

Cover, John Mitchell/Photo Researchers; 2–3, ©Jens Wolf/Corbis; 4, Kathrin Ayer; 4–5, ©Daniel Heuclin/NHPA; 6, ©James Gerholdt/NHPA; 7BKG, ©Jan Vermeer/Foto Natura/Minden Pictures; 8, ©Jon Triffo; 9, ©John Mitchell/Photo Researchers; 10, ©Doug Cheeseman/Peter Arnold; 11, ©Stanley A. Schultz and Marguerite J. Schultz, *The Tarantula Keeper's Guide*, Barron's, 1998, p. 211; 12–13, ©Daniel Heuclin/NHPA; 14–15, ©James Gerholdt; 16, ©Jon Triffo; 17, ©Wernher Krutein/Photovault.com; 18–19, ©Wernher Krutein/Photovault.com; 20, ©Martin Harvey/NHPA; 21, ©Robert Mitchell; 22L, ©David Hosking/Corbis; 22C, ©Robert Mitchell; 22R, ©Anthony Bannister/Corbis; 23TL, ©James Gerholdt/NHPA; 23TR, ©Jacques Jangoux/Peter Arnold; 23BL, ©Jon Triffo; 23BR, ©John Bell/Bruce Coleman; 23BKG, ©James Gerholdt.

Publisher: Kenn Goin
Editorial Director: Adam Siegel
Editorial Development: Nancy Hall, Inc.
Creative Director: Spencer Brinker
Photo Researcher: Carousel Research, Inc.: Mary Teresa Giancoli
Design: Otto Carbajal

Library of Congress Cataloging-in-Publication Data

Goldish, Meish.
  Goliath bird-eating tarantula : the world's biggest spider / by Meish Goldish.
      p. cm.—(SuperSized!)
  Includes bibliographical references (p.   ) and index.
  ISBN-13: 978-1-59716-389-7 (lib. bdg.)
  ISBN-10: 1-59716-389-9 (lib. bdg.)
  1. Tarantulas—Juvenile literature. I. Title.

QL458.42.T5G65 2007
595.4'4—dc22

                    2006028816

For more information, write to Bearport Publishing Company, Inc., 101 Fifth Avenue, Suite 6R, New York, New York 10003. Printed in the United States of America.

10 9 8 7 6 5 4 3 2 1

Contents

A Giant Creeper

The Goliath bird-eating **tarantula** is the biggest spider in the world.

Even its name is big!

A Goliath bird-eating tarantula is about as big as a dinner plate or a Frisbee.

A Goliath bird-eating tarantula can grow up to 11 inches (27.9 cm) long.

Home in a Hole

The Goliath bird-eating tarantula lives in the **rain forests** of South America.

It makes its home in a **burrow** deep in the ground.

Some Goliaths dig their own burrows.

Other Goliaths move into burrows left by other animals.

When a tarantula becomes too big for its burrow, it leaves. The spider finds a new burrow or digs a bigger one.

burrow

Goliath Bird-Eating Tarantulas in the Wild

Atlantic Ocean

Pacific Ocean

South America

Where Goliath bird-eating tarantulas live

Eating Big

The Goliath bird-eating tarantula eats big and small creatures.

It can eat mice, lizards, frogs, or snakes.

Sometimes this tarantula even eats birds.

That's how the giant spider got its name!

fangs

A Goliath bird-eating tarantula bites victims with its deadly **fangs.** The fangs are about 1 inch (2.5 cm) long.

bird

Laying Eggs

A Goliath mother lays more than 100 eggs at a time.

She keeps them in a bag of silk that she makes.

The mother watches her eggs at all times.

silk bag of eggs

A Goliath mother takes her eggs with her when she leaves her burrow.

Growing Fast

Goliath spiders hatch from their eggs after six or seven weeks.

The baby spiders grow up fast.

They leave home after just a few weeks.

After a baby hatches, it digs its own burrow.

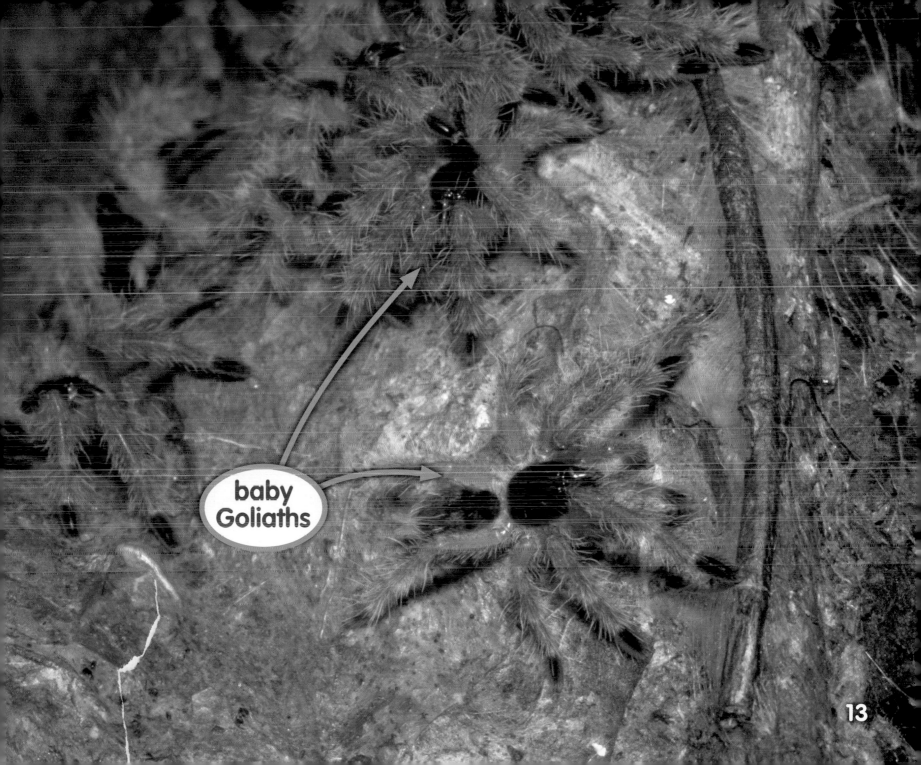

baby
Goliaths

A New Skin

As it grows, the Goliath bird-eating tarantula gets too big for its skin.

So it sheds its old skin.

The new skin is soft and takes time to harden.

The spider grows new skin many times during its life.

A Goliath tarantula grows back a leg if it loses one.

Helpful Hairs

The Goliath spider is covered with long, dark hairs.

The spider uses its hairs to feel things moving nearby.

A Goliath spider has eight eyes but sees poorly. It uses its hairs to feel its way around.

eyes

Loud and Scary

A Goliath bird-eater may rub its hairy legs together if an enemy is near.

The rubbing makes a hissing sound.

The noise can be heard 15 feet (4.6 m) away!

It scares away most enemies.

The Goliath can flick some of its hairs at an enemy. The stiff hairs sting.

Rain Forest Survivors

Male Goliath bird-eaters live about 5 years.

Females may live more than 20 years.

People build homes on the spiders' rain forest land.

Yet these tough tarantulas still find places to survive.

Tarantulas are among the longest living spiders.

Glossary

burrow
(BUR-oh) a hole
or tunnel in the
ground made by
an animal for it
to live in

rain forests
(RAYN FOR-ists)
large areas of land
covered with trees
and plants, where
lots of rain falls

fangs
(FANGZ)
long, sharp,
pointed teeth

tarantula
(tuh-RAN-chuh-luh)
a hairy, large
spider that lives
mainly in warm
areas

Index

Read More

Cooper, Jason. *Tarantulas.* Vero Beach, FL: Rourke Publishing (2005).

Facklam, Margery. *Spiders and Their Web Sites.* Boston, MA: Little, Brown (2001).

Markle, Sandra. *Spiders: Biggest! Littlest!* Honesdale, PA: Boyds Mills Press (2004).

Learn More Online

To learn more about Goliath bird-eating tarantulas, visit

www.bearportpublishing.com/SuperSized